The Freight Broker Book

A 21st Century Training Guide to Running a
Successful Freight Brokerage Business Startup From
Scratch

By

Forrest Rhodes

Disclaimer

This publication is designed to provide competent and reliable information regarding the subject matter covered. However, the views expressed in this publication are those of the author alone, and should not be taken as expert instruction or professional advice. The reader is responsible for his or her own actions.

The author hereby disclaims any responsibility or liability whatsoever that is incurred from the use or application of the contents of this publication by the purchaser or reader. The purchaser or reader is hereby responsible for his or her own actions.

Table of Contents

Introduction

The freight brokerage industry is a thriving industry, but you can soar amidst unrelenting competitors if you have the right skill, knowledge, and experience. Freight brokerage takes a long process and involves multi personnel to get goods transported from one place to the other. At the top of the list is a freight broker.

A freight broker facilitates the process and connects everyone involved in the process of goods transportation. In the pages of this book, we have explained who a freight broker is – his job description and traits. If you intend to be a freight broker or you are already one, this book will lead you through all the twists and turns in the career path. It gives you a rundown of what you should expect and be prepared for.

In this book, you will find all that you need.

I welcome you to dive in!

Chapter 1

Basics of The Freight Brokerage Industry

Who Is a Freight Broker?

Basically, a freight broker can be an individual or a company that helps a shipper and motor carrier achieve their goals.

How?

They find a shipper that needs transport to disperse goods and merge him with a registered motor carrier that wants to render the service.

They are what you'll call transportation intermediary, which simply means they are not an asset-owning carrier or a shipper, but only serve as a middle man in the movement of cargo. Freight Brokers ate indispensable because they provide an important service to shippers and carriers. They assist carriers by filling the trucks and earning a certain commission for their services. They assist shippers in finding genuine motor carriers, that they (the shippers) might have no clue about how to locate.

The Players

It takes a committed and vibrant team for an industry to thrive. It happens that some of the duties of the teammates might overlap. Nevertheless, no one is irrelevant in the industry.

The following key players and their responsibilities are listed below.

Shipper: An individual or company that has goods and wants to transport them.

Freight Broker: A personnel or company that serves as a middle man and connects shippers and carriers.

Freight Forwarder: Majority mix them up with freight brokers. They are remarkably different. They receive goods and consolidate several smaller shipments into one big shipment. Then, they make arrangements to transport the larger shipment using several shipping methods- water, air and land carriers.

Shipper's associations: They are nonprofit organizations that are made up of shippers with the aim to decrease transportation costs by pooling shipments. Their operations are similar to freight forwarders. However, their service is exclusive to their members alone and not for the public.

Agricultural Truck Broker: They are somewhat small and operate in an area in the country. They provide motor carrier service for agricultural products.

Motor Carrier: This is a company that renders truck transportation services. They provide truck transportation. It can be private or hire. A private motor carrier provides truck transportation of its own cargo, while a hire motor carrier provides truck transportation of cargo that belongs to others.

Import-Export Broker: They are basically facilitators for importers and exporters. They interface with international carriers, government agencies and other entities that are equally involved in international freight transportation.

In a perfect world, of course, each entity in the industry would handle its traditional role and that's all. However, the transportation industry is changing so rapidly that once-distinctive lines are blurring. Also, it's quite common for a successful freight broker to create subsidiaries that provide other freight services.

History of Freight Brokering

When you visit a freight broker's office or company, the uninterrupted buzzing fax machine, continuous ringing of the telephone to engaged conversations can make you think that freight brokering has been existing for years. However, in freight training school, you will get to understand it is a current and modern update in the logistics world. The roots of freight brokering can be traced back to the history of the trucking industry in the U.S.

Prior to the availability of trucks and tractor-trailers, the job of moving freights for local shipments was carried out by train or a horse-drawn carriage. Trains were reserved for transporting goods to major cities. In the early 1900s, trucks were limited to short routes, more so because their engines were fueled by electricity. Driving was tedious and lengthy because there were no paved roads in the countryside. Thus making trucks only confined to transporting small goods within the city. In 1910, there was a rapt growth in technological innovations in the transporting industry, with the availability of gasoline-powered engines, tractors and semi-trailer combinations made for wider roads. This spiked up an increase in the popularity of moving freight by truck. Nevertheless, the poor road condition of rural areas and solid tires, plus the speed limit of 15mph posed a huge restriction for trucks in the cities.

Trucks gained more exposure to hauling freight in the second world war, due to the congestion of trains and railways. During this period, everyone including shippers and the government started exploring long-distance truck shipments. With the invention of pneumatic tires, faster speeds were achieved.

Additionally, in 1930, the availability of paved roads made it possible for trucks to go farther. In 1960, the US built an interstate highway system that linked cities and towns in the US. At this time, trucking could deliver goods at any place and time. It was making waves in the transportation industry, with an unshaken dominance in the freight industry.

In 1935, the Motor Carrier Act passed by congress disrupted certain things- unknown and upcoming players couldn't enter the market easily.

However, In 1980, things took a different twist, as the deregulation of the trucking industry paved way for new players. For instance, trucking companies were offering warehousing services and warehousing companies were getting involved in freight shipment.

This was achieved by lobbying and hard work on the part of some industry stakeholders.

This lead to the influx of small businesses into the logistics world, birthing competition amongst them and established companies.

The happy consequence of the new development was decreased shipping rates. Shippers were able to shop for excellent and trustworthy carriers. Manufacturers also were able to ship their products to any distance, regardless of the distance. As a result of all this, freight brokers began to gain relevance and fame. Manufacturers depended on them to deliver goods to their customers on time.

The industry began to thrive and flourish. Freight brokers liaised between shipper and carrier. Thus, ensuring that shipments get to the consignees.

Future Projections

No doubt, the freight brokerage industry has been on the frontline of the transportation industry over the years. The industry has experienced tremendous growth and keeps growing every minute. The success of freight brokerage industry provides an avenue for customer and the carrier to enjoy their value-added services.

In the process of collecting the supply and demand sides of the shipping industry, they have earned an estimated $40/billion in revenue in the previous year. And, it will grow in the following year

Of late, two years exactly, there have been some transition in the capitalist operations regarding freight brokerage services. Key players in the area of technology have designed various applications and tools for the virtual delivery of services between customers and clients.

The new move of a digital approach in the industry can be attributed to the latest technology growths in the various silos of transportation. The prevalence of self-driving trucks helps reduces costs and boost efficiencies to accurately predicting freight and shipping analytic software that taps the power of large data, thus making customers and carriers to be independent of third-party intermediaries.

The distribution of new technologies also comes with its challenges, including capital that is required to replace or supplement existing legacy systems and slow adoption. Nevertheless, technology companies keep surmounting these challenges.

The changes sweeping through the freight and transportation industry must not be trivialized by freight brokers regardless of their location, market sphere or niche. They need to adapt to the new environment and situation as it comes and be proactive in the process.

They must embrace the technology that is presently available at their disposal. This wave of new technology reduces hassles, makes communication effective, saves time and provides good data that helps in boosting processes in-house, and provides value-quality services

Another great way to prepare for the changes is to improve on the relationships with their present customers and partners because technology can never replace the human touch aspect of the business. This can be achieved by getting feedback from customers and carriers and implementing them.

Essentially, freight brokers can welcome these changes and embrace the opportunities they bring.

Benefits of Being a Freight Broker

1. It breeds independence.

As a freight broker, you call the shots. You determine how you choose to start and groom your business You can decide to start as a one-man operation or have two or more employees. You don't have to report back to any boss. You own and make your own decisions. It's rare to come across a high-paid job that comes with this kind of independence. As a result of this, you can take responsibility for your decisions and run your business the way you desire, without any external influence.

2. Freight brokers spend more quality time with their families.

All jobs come with their requirements and hazards. You'll agree with me that most high-paying jobs are time-consuming and require attention. However, as a freight broker, you choose your working time and mode of operations. This provides flexibility that doesn't come with other professions. You can always create time to spend with your families from your flexible schedule. It's exciting that as you grow in your career, you also carry your family along and have good and beautiful memories together. It's a known fact that having a happy family is one of the secrets of a successful career. This means, when your family is happy and you are glad to always go home, it positively affects your career. As a broker, you can enjoy a thriving career and a beautiful family altogether.

3. It's highly profitable.

Freight brokers earn so much money. If you have a trucking company, you should add freight broker service to streamline your trucking operations and work on improving your customer care services, rather than allowing other freight brokers to cut into the revenue you can enjoy bountifully alone.

4. It's affordable to set up.

Generally, freight brokers have low start-up costs. So long you have a good credit standing, you don't need more than $3,500 to start In this industry. A lot of well-known freight brokers started their careers with the dining table doubling as a workspace. You can start from the comfort of your home, and move to a larger space when you have more clients.

5. It's easy to maintain.

It's one thing to start a business, it's another thing to maintain it. Most business owners are unable to run their business after a while, due to huge overhead expenses. As a freight broker, you are not required to spend so much on your overhead expense.

6. You can earn as much as you desire

The good thing about being a freight broker is that you can earn as much as you want. Because the industry keeps growing every day and businesses are emerging daily, there's always an exchange of goods on a daily basis. This could only mean you are provided with more opportunities to earn more. Therefore, the only limitation to your income is your drive and commitment to your business.

7. It is a valuable legacy.

You want a business that can not only take care of your family needs but one that transcends one generation to the other. There's no other investment that can do this than freight brokering.

Once you are grounded in the industry, you can get your children Involved and passing on the legacy in the process.

8. It's easy to diversify.

As a freight broker, you are your own boss and you can manage your time, and resources whichever way you like. It's very easy to diversify into other enterprises or expand as much as you want because of the independence you have on the job.

You can choose to expand at your own pace and in other areas.

9. It offers job stability and security.

One of the greatest fear of most employees is losing their job. Most times, even entrepreneurs get worried about the future of their business. This is not the case of a freight broker. Simply because freight brokerage offers job security like no other. You are your own boss and you can't be scared of anyone laying you off.

10. They don't go out of season.

Typically, some careers thrive in certain seasons of the year or period. This is not the case for freight brokers, you make origin all-round the year – day in and out.

Chapter 2

Becoming A Freight Broker

You do not become a successful freight broker in a day. It takes lots of knowledge and experience to be good at the job.

You need to know your roles and responsibilities as a freight broker, so you don't get distracted by other duties. A freight broker has lots of responsibilities. However, we have complied the major and essential roles of a freight broker in this chapter.

Additionally, you must know the basic traits of a freight broker. These are attributes that you must imbibe for you to carry out your duties effectively.

Roles And Responsibilities of Freight Brokers

Typically, freight brokers have four major responsibilities which includes:

1. Facilitating the passage of shipments from the shipper to the carrier.

2. Preparation of documentation and reports involved in the transportation of goods.

3. Negotiation and settlement of all monetary obligations.

4. Sourcing for customers and truckers, and ensuring that the present clients are satisfied with the service provided.

Drilling down to what these roles and responsibilities would translate to, the following tasks may be part of your daily routine as a freight broker:

1. Working with clients to conclude on an ideal rate for a specific load ad ensuring that your commission is included.
2. Searching for carriers or truckers that can do deliveries to the consignee.
3. Preparing the necessary documentation and load information that is required for each cargo, using the right system and software.
4. Monitoring load movement by been in regular contact with shippers and drivers to ensure that the shipment is delivered on time.
5. Arrangement of load storage, if the need arises.
6. Effective handling of problems that may arise in the process of goods delivery

7. Confirming from truckers and consignees if your load has been delivered according to the time frame and load information

8. Sending bills to shippers and paying your carriers per time with appropriate documentation.

9. Networking with the right individuals, carriers, companies and stakeholders in your field to grow your new business

10. Drafting the appropriate marketing materials to build your business.

Basic Traits of a Freight Broker

These are the important traits that a good freight broker must possess.

1. **Optimistic and Self-motivated.**

   To be a successful freight broker, you must be highly optimistic and passionate about what you do. The motivation will help you get through the job. It's impossible that you will work with people that have the same traits as you.

   Be prepared for disappointments, delays, and difficult clients. Along the line, it's easy to get discouraged and give up. However, when you are optimistic and have a positive outlook towards your job, you will be able to soar above any challenges that knock on the door.

2. **Results-Oriented.**

To succeed in the industry, you must be able to set goals and map out strategies to achieve the goals.

It's been noted that setting targets and milestones towards achieving the goals of your company.

You must set weekly, monthly and yearly goals and map out strategies to carry out the tasks. Your goals will keep you focused and make you disciplined.

3. **Strategic.**

The job of a freight brokerage is enormous and involves lots of details. It's easy to lose sight of your purpose if you are not strategic in your approach.

As a successful freight broker, you must have a strategic mindset repeatedly to review and learn new things. You must also be updated about the happenings in the industry to be able to adjust to changes that arise.

4. **Proactive.**

In the process of moving loads from shipper to consignee, a lot of things take place at the same time. You must be able to foresee problems ahead and have a diverse response mechanism to address issues.

You should be able to handle certain situations – when a truck is faulty or an accident occurs.

You must always have a plan A, plan B, and other plans subsequently.

5. **Decisive.**

Because you have so much task ahead as a freight broker, you must be decisive in your making decisions and in carrying out your tasks. You should prioritize your tasks and know what is important and what should come last.

6. **Exceptionally Customer Oriented.**

As a freight broker, you will have lots of clients. You must be devoted to satisfying your clients and ensuring that their needs are met. Your customer's feedback is very important and should be of high priority.

7. **Flexibility.**

The ability to multitask is very important. You must be able to be flexible enough to handle a lot of the work rudiments and the changes that come with the job.

8. **Ability To Sustain Relationships.**

You must be able to build and nurture relationships to be able to have a thriving freight brokerage business. You will meet lots of people on the job, and you must continually maintain helpful, healthy, and vital relationships.

Work Routine of a Freight Broker

Just like every job, a freight broker have a work routine. Your work routine may change depending on your number of clients, employees and the size of your organization. You must be familiar with the work routine so that you don't skip any important step in carrying out your task.

This is a simple and detailed work routine of any freight broker.

1. The broker will start the day by requesting for the order simply by calling shippers early in the morning (usually from 7:30 am -10:30 am). That is

when the shippers will tidy up things on their needs. Typically, the broker will be asking if the shipper is looking for trucks on that specific day. If the response is negative, the broker moves on to the next person, until he is satisfied with anyone or several. And, he springs into action.

Afterward, the shipper will be the one initiating calls to the broker, rather than the broker calling the shipper.

2. The second stage involves taking the order from the shipper. The shipper will explain in detail the requirement. At this point, the broker should let his reservations and uncertainties be known. Also, the broker must give the carrier the right information when they call.

3. Usually, the broker can work up the estimate of the price rate and give the shipper the information later or the broker can ask the shipper how much they'd like to pay. Although profits can be more, the ideal thing is to get at least 10% profit margins on each load. Afterward, the next step is to ensure the loads are posted on the internet load boards.

4. When the loads are posted, the broker will go to his database of available trucks and call each carrier to know if there are available trucks. At this point, the broker may also be getting calls from people who have seen the posts on the load boards

5. Then, the broker starts looking for a dispatcher or driver. As soon as the broker gets a positive response from the carrier, he or she reaches out to the shipper to inform them that the Load is covered.

6. The broker will send their setup package to the carrier through fax or email. The carrier will start processing the papers and the broker will make findings about the carrier to ensure the carrier is authorized and insured. The broker may use the internet or telephone or a third party for this purpose.

7. Afterward, the carrier will get a confirmation. And he/she will sign the document and send it back to the broker.

8. As soon as the broker gets the confirmation, the broker will reach out to the driver. Sometimes, the driver may have already called the broker.

The information of the load is given to the drive, alongside relevant instructions.

9. Once the load has been delivered and the carrier has given the broker feedback, the broker will reach out to the shipper to inform them of the status.

10. Problems like delivery failure, missing goods, or damaged goods must be handled between the carrier and shipper. In some cases, the broker may intervene, but the broker is not liable for damages, except the broker is careless.

11. Finally, when the load is delivered appropriately, the broker repeats the same process every now and then.

The routine of a broker may seem basic, and boring, but it's far from the truth. Sometimes, the broker has a pleasant experience on the job. Other times, the broker encounters diverse challenges.

Challenges like missing goods, late deliveries, delays, and more.

It is inevitable to encounter these problems, but it's important to be in charge and always ready to tackle these problems articulately.

Training and Experience

For you to become a licensed freight broker, you need to acquire the necessary training. Vast experience in shipping, trucking, or logistics is quite helpful. It helps you lay a solid foundation for a promising career as a freight broker. Nevertheless, there are equally classes and courses you must pursue for you to get a clear and detailed understanding of the industry.

Sometimes, the training opportunities are not legally required for you to be a freight broker. However, they provide you with the right information on the happenings and trends in the industry, work ethics, practices, and technology software and tools.

Lots of freight broker training schools offer lessons and coursework to people who desire to work as freight brokers. Certain schools provide a personalized curriculum, while some are self-study classes online. You should choose the best training school and class you want to enroll in so that you can get your freight brokerage business thriving.

On The Job Training

One great way to get freight broker training is through other roles in the industry. For instance, when you work as a truck driver, it gives you a detailed glimpse of the trucking world.

Below are few examples.

- Shipping logistics firm: This is similar to the role of a dispatcher. A logistic firm does the planning and execution movements of cargo in the supply chain.

- Truck Driver: As a truck driver, you can have first-hand experience of what a truck experiences daily when delivering cargo.

- Dispatcher with a trucking company: Generally, they coordinate and control the driver routes and schedules. They also communicate the status updates with the various shippers

Gain Industry Insights

You can acquire more knowledge by studying the industry meticulously. Things are changing every day. The logistics, shipping and transportation industry keeps shifting every year.

When you get acquainted with the changes, it enables you to serve your clients and customers well, and pre/vents legal issues with new laws.

For starters, leading publications on shipping, logistics, trucking and online forums are where you can start from.

You can also reach out to fellow freight brokers and others in the industry to get more info about the trends in the industry.

Take A Freight Broker Class (Online Vs. On-location)

There are lots of online, on-location, and offline freight broker training schools to enroll in. Some online freight broker schools can be highly beneficial. For instance, Freight broker planet has a huge advantage if you have a tight schedule or can't commute to a school. However, on-location training offers better one on one attention and hands-on training. It's essential for learning programs to teach you the core principles that you need to learn in becoming a freight broker.

Choosing The Right Training Program

It's paramount that you assess the available training programs based on your present knowledge and experience in the field.

Spend time revising what you know and decide on the skills you need to improve on. That way, it's easier to know the freight school that you need to attend.

As soon as you identify with your educational needs, you need to decide if you will take courses at a physical location or you will prefer an online version. You can check the locations of the major schools that offer this training and see which works for you.

But, if there's no school in your proximity, then you can opt for the online version.

Finally, you should know how much time you want to invest in a training program and the budget that is required of you. There are lots of programs with different time duration and prices.

Recommended Training Programs

You need several skills and knowledge in all areas including sales, marketing and communication to excel as a freight broker.

Here's a list of top freight broker schools to enroll in.

1. Broker U

Udemy has a brokering class called Broker U.

You can check their website below

Website: https://www.udemy.com/broker-u-gateway-to-becoming-a-freight-broker/

2. Freight Broker Bootcamp

This is a well-embraced online platform for freight broker training. The website contains the information you need.

Website: http://www.freightbrokerbootcamp.com/

3. Rapid Authority

This school is good for those that are close to Southeast of the US.

Not only do they offer workshops on how to start your freight brokering business, they also provide licensing help services.

Website: http://www.rapid-authority.com/

4. Freight Broker Agent School

As a newbie, you can take courses at Freight Broker Agent School. The courses and workshops are organized in Georgia and Florida.

Website: http://www.freightbrokeragentschool.com/

5. Atex Freight Broker Training

You can take the courses online, from any part of the world. And if you are interested, there are in-class programs you can also participate in.

Website: http://atexfreightbrokertraining.com/

Chapter 3

Freight Brokerage Business Startup

Choose The Right Legal Structure

To develop a business plan, you must choose a business structure that is recognized legally either by the federal or state government. What differentiates each framework is liability and taxes.

The main types of business structures that can be used in setting up your freight brokerage business are discussed briefly below.

Limited Liability Corporation (LLC)

An LLC is a business framework whose legal liability is passed to the business rather than the owner of the business. Any profits and losses recorded in the business are channeled via the LLC structure to personal income – there is no need of paying corporate taxes. Nonetheless, the owners of the business pay self-employment taxes.

Partnership

Here, two or more people can set up a legal business structure. Profits realized in such a business set up are channeled via the partnership structure to personal income, just like an LLC. A limited partnership or a limited liability partnership can be created, with each having its advantages and disadvantages to the concerned partners.

Sole Proprietorship

Here, only a single owner of the business exists. The assets and liabilities of the business are not separated from the assets and liabilities that are personal. Therefore, the owner of the business is responsible for all incurred debts. This simple structure is accompanied with tax and legal complications.

Corporation (S or C)

C and S corporations are additional options new freight brokers can opt for.

- **C corp** is a business structure that exists individually from its owners. This option provides the best protection from personal liability.

- **S corp** though similar is meant to prevent double taxation encountered by C corp. Profits and some losses incurred under S corp are channeled via the business owners and not having to be subjected to corporate taxes.

Location of Your Business

One of the most fascinating thing about a freight brokerage business is that your physical startup requirements are not outrageous or demanding.

Compared to a freight forwarder or carrier, you don't need a warehouse or loading dock. You necessarily don't need a fancy office , because your customers aren't likely to come to your location,

You must understand that where you choose to operate from depends on certain factors – goals and available resources. Lots of brokers start from the comfort of their homes with the intention of moving into commercial space when they have more clients.

The advantage of starting from home is that it reduces the cost of startup and the capital that will be required. Nevertheless, you must consider other factors aside from the upfront cash that you'll need. Do you have a spare room in your home? Can you have enough privacy to work, when you are at home?

Although, starting in a commercial setting needs more capital than starting from home. However, you can have an efficient and productive setup than using your bedroom.

Choose a Business Name and Register Your Business

For you to successfully run a freight brokerage business, you need to choose a suitable company name and register your business with the appropriate authorities.

Ensure that you check if the name you have chosen is already taken at the Us Patent and Trademark office at https://www.uspto.gov/.

Registering your name also involves choosing the kind of entity you would like to register as

- Limited Liability Company.
- Partnership.
- Corporation.
- Sole Proprietor

Afterward, you must ensure that you register your business in the state you reside in, at your local business license department to conclude this step.

Develop a Business Plan

You must prepare a quality and air-tight business plan if you are keen on starting a freight brokerage business.

Having a business plan helps you put in an application for a loan with your bank but even more so, your business plan is a blueprint that specifies your target niche and your customers.

Your business plan is your go-to strategy and as you figure out the specifics and research the market of your business, the more prepared you will be to meet the challenges of your business.

You can use the business plan template below which is designed for freight brokers.

A. Executive Summary

This section is usually the last bit of information supplied on your business plan because it provides an insight into what your business is all about. Mostly two pages long, it provides a summary of all key points addressed in the sections below. However, don't be fooled by the length because in most cases, it is the portion of your presentation that can either make or mar you when seeking for investors or when applying for a loan. The strength of your Executive Summary is what investors or loan lenders will scan through before taking a leap of faith in you.

B. Description of Business and Vision

Here, whoever reads your business plan will have a solid understanding of the business and what it represents. This section is also where you provide insights on the growth of the business and its potential.

Subheadings:

- Mission Statement
- The vision of the Business
- Business Goals and Objectives
- A Short History of the Business
- List of Main Company Principals

C. Market Definition

Defining your market involves deciding the niche of your market, knowing your customers and the likely reach of your freight brokerage business.

Below are some questions you have to answer:

- What industry do you function in and what are are its prospects?

- What are your freight brokerage business scope and its potential market share?

- What market segments will you be targeting?

- What problems and needs of customers will you be addressing?

- Who are your target customers?

- Who are your key rivals?

Subheadings:

- Industry of the Business and its Outlook

- Pressing Needs of Potential or Existing Market

- Target Market

- Persona of the Customer

- Market Share

- Competitive Intelligence

- Profiles of Key Rivals

D. Service Description

This section is where you separate your service from other competitors. Upon reading this section of your business plan, your potential investor should have a solid grasp of your business and why you are into it.

Subheadings:

- Service Description
- Strategy for Pricing
- Competitive Edge

E. Strategic Direction

Here, the SWOT analysis is performed. What you typically do here is to understudy the strengths, weaknesses, opportunities and threats of your business vis-à-vis your target market, your market industry, and in general, the larger economy among others.

This section is sometimes included by some in the market assessment or products and services section of a business plan, while some opt to differentiate it to provide further drilling on the success factors of the freight brokerage business.

Subheadings:

- The Freight Brokerage Business Strengths

- Weaknesses

- Market Opportunities

- Threats

- New Services (such as services to offer in the future)

- Future Goals and Objectives of the Business (e.g., transforming the business into a franchise)

F. Marketing and Sales Strategy

This discusses how you intend to market and grow your business. Discuss the marketing means you will adopt be it web strategy, advertising, public relations, and so on. Moreso, you need to drill down on who you are targeting, how you intend to reach them, and how you intend to competitively sell your services.

A subsection on aligning with strategic partners should be catered for such as those you will be working with to discover new and serve existing customers.

Your networking efforts should also be discussed—how, when and where.

Subheadings:

- Description of the Market

- Service Demand
- Strategy for Marketing
- Strategy for Promotions
- Strategy for Sales
- Strategy for Web and Internet Marketing
- Strategic Alliances

G. Organization and Management

The operational flow of your freight brokerage business will need to be defined such as work flows, record keeping, billing and accounting among others. The business routines should be outlined, likewise your business legalities. Also, list the principles of the business and their roles and responsibilities.

Subheadings:

- Form of Ownership
- Management Team and their Roles and Responsibilities
- Structure of the Organization
- Plan for Personnel (Including freight agents)
- Legal Process Agents and States of Operation

- Legal Representative

H. Financial Management

This is the numbers-crunching section and for most people, the least liked. However, this is one key area most perceived investors and loan lenders will focus on because one of their concerns will be to know the financial viability of your business and its future projections.

As a new entrant in the freight brokerage business, an estimate of your start-up costs, and the projected numbers for your operation in the coming year should be shown. Use this for this purpose; balance sheet, income statement, and cash flow statement.

On the other hand, if your business has been existing for some time but you are seeking for new investors or loans, use the balance sheets and income statements to show your last 3 years' reports from your business operations. A cash flow statement will also need to be provided. For loans, loan managers would like to get a copy of your principal's personal financial statements and the previous year's tax forms.

Subheadings (where applicable):

- Start-Up Costs

- Projected/Current Statement of Income
- Projected/Current Cash Flow Statement
- Projected/Current Balance Sheet
- Business Principals' Personal Financial Statements
- Previous Year Federal Tax Returns

As seen already, spending quality time preparing a business plan for your business will help you manage your business productively and in a more disciplined way. However, this plan is not the end of it, it should be dynamic and revisited to reflect changes in trends, current economics, and realities among others.

Find Your Carriers

A freight broker without carriers is likened to a ship without sails.

As a freight broker, one of your marketing skills should include finding carriers who are skilled and experienced in the field. There are several ways to find your carries such as online directories, networking events and direct recommendations and references. Let's take a look at more options.

Cold Calling

Finding a freight carrier you will like to use makes it simple to find a contact number in a business listing. Do not attempt to sell your business as the best broker when you call, instead describe what your needs are, e.g., load sizes needed for transportation, places the freight will be moved to, and the frequency of loads. This is what impressed several people in the logistic business and not empty promises. Also, showing interest in the current means a freight carrier transports their freights will go a long way in getting your first freight carrier.

Develop Personal Relationships

To thrive in the transportation business, you need to build a cordial business relationship. You will have to get along really well with shippers, consignees, and carriers to succeed. You will even have to imbibe their values and if you do, you are good to get a carrier for your business especially because carriers will more likely talk to other carriers about you.

Leads With Day-Day Products

Several products around you were at some time freights and conveyed on a truck, such as office furniture, and cars, conveyed by truck. Simply research the products you utilize daily. Inquire about the location of their manufacturing and how they are transported to their destination.

One quick way to find carriers is to look up the products you once ordered. To uncover carrier names, take a look at the tracking number, bills of lading, or other shipping information. Doing this will help you locate local carriers with a contract to bigger networks, thus enlarging your options.

Using The Internet

More carriers now value having a presence on the web. Internet load boards exist that can help you to discover a limitless supply of great carriers. You will have to work with the best carriers if you want to build a solid network.

Take Note of Other Methods of Transportation

A noteworthy place for freight brokers is the truckload motor carrier services. However, other shipping methods exist such as air freight and rail. Keeping these shipping options at the back of your mind could help you to find a carrier faster.

Income & Pricing Strategy

Generally, Freight charges are influenced by certain factors - distance and weight of the load. Most times, the rates are also affected by the type of truck that will be used for shipping, and the number of stops for pick up or delivery of goods.

You generate income by the commissions you get on each load. You can be paid by billing the shipper the amount you will be paying the carrier plus the total amount of your commission, or by billing the shipper directly and you are paid a commission from its revenue.

The common and popular way to handle billing and commission issues is to let the carrier bill you and you bill your customers subsequently.

Chapter 4

Getting the Required Paperwork

Being a freight broker will require you to get down with so much paperwork- it's not something you can avoid. And this is quite understandable because like a lot of banking transactions, you will find yourself in the middle of countless transactions and endless paper trails. There are samples online on some of the forms you can make use of, but it's best you create your own paperwork. Freight brokers who are more experienced advise that you come up with your own forms, contractions to suit your mode of operation. It's a piece of great advice because there are operational preferences, every freight broker operation is unique.

Carrier/Broker Agreement

One of the agreements you need to make as a freight broker after you match a load to be shipped by a carrier is the carrier/broker agreement. Basically, this agreement indicates the terms and conditions that bind your work together with the given carrier. It comprises all the dealings that will exist between you and the carrier, with provisions for any possible changes in the future.

There are some things you need to put into consideration when creating a carrier/broker agreement as given below:

1. Make sure you indicate the carrier license number or MC (Motor Carrier), together with the full name and address of the carrier.

2. If your dealings with the carrier are on a contract basis, indicate that negotiations will be carried out for the freight and rates for every shipment.

3. Indicate that any loss or damage to the freight when it's been transported will be covered by the carrier.

4. Indicate that if the freight suffers any injury or damage while in the carrier's possession, then it is the responsibility of the carrier to fix it.

5. Indicate when the carrier will get paid and state certain things the carrier is mandated to provide before payment.

Confirmation of Load and Agreement of Rate

As soon as a carrier consents to move a load, you are required to respond by sending a load confirmation and rate agreement form. In this form, you should have the name and address of the shipper and the consignee, a tracking number, any additional information on stops, a short description of the item being shipped, pick up and delivery dates, and your payment or fee structure.

Bill of Lading

When the driver comes to pick up the item, the shipper is required to give a bill of lading. The form contains information like the nature and size of the load, where it's headed and any other additional information for example- if it is a fragile load. The driver will sign the bill of lading as a form of acknowledgment for the load received.

As a broker, you wouldn't really need to be concerned with this document, but you will still need to have a signed copy in your possession. This form is often prepared and exchanged by the shipper and the carrier. After it's been signed, the form and the invoice for the transport services will be sent to you by the carrier.

Labor Receipt for Contractor

For ease and smooth unloading, drivers may use the services of contract laborers. The laborers will help unload trucks as soon as they get to the consignee.

If the services of contract laborers are used, the driver will be given a contract labor receipt. Then the driver or the carrier pays for their services and later sends the document to you for reimbursement. You'll notify the shipper concerning the payment. But if the shipper is not willing to pay, you should foot the bill to sustain the relationships you have with the carrier and the driver.

Invoicing

You will be sent an invoice together with the bill of lading once the delivery is done and confirmed by the carrier. After receiving the documents, you can then create your own invoice to be sent to the shipper, that's if the carrier does not bill the shipper directly.

Your invoice will contain information like the dates of pick up and delivery, the billing date, the origin and the destination, the item shipped with its full description (like the weights, number e.t.c), additional charges (for example the contract labor fees or excess weight). Basically, you need to send your bill to the shipper as soon as you get the bill of lading and invoice from your carrier. There are some cases where you will need to bill the consignee instead of the shipper, all you need to do is get adequate information concerning the payment of the shipment.

Contract of Carriage

A lot of brokers see the bill of lading as a contract of carriage, but this is actually not true. The bill of lading does not contain lots of elements required by any contract, but it is an element found in a contract of carriage.

It's not like a contract of carriage is a document on its own. A contract of carriage is made up of the bill of lading, law binding rules to be followed whether from the federal, state, or local level, and also rules on how the item is to be handled, pricing, additional charges and basically all the services to be provided.

Managing Your Records

It's important that you know how to manage and maintain good records for every transaction. Apart from the normal information of shippers and carriers in your possession, you will still have to record every transaction. And each record should have the following information:

1. The full details of the shipper; like the name and address

2. Details of the originating motor carrier; like the full name, address and registration number

3. Freight bill number or bill of laden

4. The fees received by the broker for his services and the name of the payer

5. A full detail on all brokerage services carried out together with each shipment or any other activity; the amount received and the name of the payer should also be included.

6. Fees paid to the broker for freight charges and the day it was paid to the carrier.

According to the code of federal regulations, you have to be really specific and detailed about the rules of record to keep. These records have to remain with you for a period of three years and everyone involved in a particular transaction has the right to review the records of that transaction.

A Short message from the Author:

Hey, I hope you are enjoying the book? I would love to hear your thoughts!

Many readers do not know how hard reviews are to come by and how much they help an author.

I would be incredibly grateful if you could take just 60 seconds to write a short review on Amazon, even if it is a few sentences!

>> Click here to leave a quick review

Thanks for the time taken to share your thoughts!

Chapter 5

Legal Requirement For Freight Brokers

You must be covered in all areas as a freight broker. Failure to do so could jeopardize your enterprise.

Like every other profession, you'll need to be certified as a freight broker to operate across your country. Here are some of the legal requirements for freight brokers:

1. MC Authority (Motor carrier number)

2. Insurance

3. Processing agents

4. BMC-84 Bond or Trust fund.

5. Unified carrier Registration

Obtain Your Operating Authority

The first thing you'll need before you launch into your operation is the Motor Carrier Operating Authority which is also your freight broker's license. To get started you'll need a USDOT number because you will need to provide the number on your OP-1 application form. For more information on how to fill this form, use this resource https://bit.ly/3bsxPVZ

After filling the application form, you will need to pay an application fee of $300- which is a one-time payment. After payment, you will need to wait for a processing time of four to six weeks.

As soon as your application is approved, you'll get a mail containing your MC number from the Federal Motor Carrier Safety Administration. Even after the approval, you will need to wait for an extra ten days because your MC number will be posted on the FMCSA Register page. Within these ten days, if anyone complains or shows some sort of disapproval concerning your registration, it will be reviewed by the FMCSA. However, if no one does then you will be given the full authority.

Get Your Processing Agents

You need a processing agent for every state your brokerage will operate in. In a situation where a claim is filed against your brokerage in a particular state, your processing agent in that state can be served papers.

In case you are wondering how you can get a processing agent, some commercial firms can help you for a fee. Also, the FMCSA has a list with adequate information on commercial firms that can provide processing agents. On the other hand, someone you prefer to work with can get trained as a freight agent.

As soon as you are done obtaining every processing agent, yourself or the commercial firm you are linked to have to submit a form known as the BOC-3. This form is also referred to as the designation of processing agents. This form needs to be submitted to the FMCSA and every state you want to operate in. According to the FMCSA, it's best to keep a copy of this document in your files after submission.

Get Your Surety Bond or Trust Fund

The surety bond also referred to as the BMV-84, and the Trust Fund also referred to as the BMC -85 are two very important decisions you will need to choose from as you make moves towards becoming a freight broker. It is a requirement you must provide. You can't bypass this process.

So which do you go for as a broker? The surety bond or the trust fund?

You are required as a broker to get one of these two as proof of your insurance coverage for at least $75,000. The major difference between the two is how you are required to pay.

The BMC-84, a surety bond allows brokers to pay a certain percentage of the $75,000 on a monthly basis or yearly premium

The BMC-85, a trust fund, requires that brokers pay the full $75,000, which becomes inaccessible afterward.

The two are quite similar and they both shield customers in a case where you don't carry out your roles as a freight broker. They are both not useful when it comes to a brokerage liability, so you may still be required to pay up for valid claims even if you choose any of these options. Lastly, they both fulfill the requirement of the FMCSA.

Let's take a deeper look at these two options

BMC-84

This is an option available for those who are just beginning on their brokerage journey and do not have enough working capital. For the surety bond, you are required to pay $75,000 on a monthly basis or yearly premium. Some certain factors determine the premium rate, factors like the stability and health of your business, e.t.c.

The companies (surety bond companies) will always carry out investigations concerning claims because they share in the liability.

To prevent non-compliance, certain federal rules and regulations guide the payment of this bond for timely and orderly payment. After you secure a surety bond, you will need to sign a legal agreement that indemnifies the company. This means you will also need to pay up every fee of all valid claims. The bond company prevents customers from suffering any loss, they are very useful in situations when claims are filed against you. You should avoid such situations though, because even if you get protected, you may have issues getting a surety bond later in the future. And this means your business can get affected or even be brought to a halt.

You can avoid claims by paying up on time, resolving conflicts quickly and following all the federal rules and regulations.

Concerning payment, your company will be evaluated and you will be charged annually based on your company's financial capabilities. Whatever charges- that is the percentage of the $75,000 they give you, will still fall under the requirement of the MAP-21 law. The percentage under this law is usually around $750- $9000 in a year.

BMC-85 Trust fund

Because of the method of payment, this option is more common among buoyant brokers and carriers. It is usually not used by newbies. For this option, you'll need to pay up the full amount of $75,000 which you can't access. You will also be required to pay up some bank chargers for the service offered. Concerning the company's liabilities, they are usually minor since claims will be paid from your trust fund. They may not be so eager to investigate claims though because it's been settled from your trust fund.

Concerning payment, you are not just paying the $75,000, you will also be required to pay an annual fee of $1500 thereabout. Before you purchase a trust fund, please ensure that the company has enough resources and they are not under-funded.

There is something called an irrevocable letter of credit, which the company can obtain on the behalf of Brokers for a fee or it can be gotten when the broker funds their trust with cash.

Get Your Unified Carrier Registration

This is a program compulsory and mandated by the federal authorities for the registrations of commercial vehicle operators who carry out interstate and international movements. On the 31st of December every year, it must be renewed.

As stated above, those required to get a UCR are state and international motor carriers. Additionally, anyone involved in the shipment of goods such as freight forwarders, brokers and many others must pay the UCR fee.

To register as a broker or lease company you will only need to pay the lowest amount, while for motor carriers their fee depends on the number of cars they have in a fleet.

If you don't Fulfil the UCR requirements, you will be fined (around $100- $5000 for starters) and your cars can be detained if you are caught by the authorities. In case your state doesn't have the UCR program, all you need to do is get the one from the nearest state because it doesn't exempt you from the law.

How to get a UCR

As soon as you've gotten your surety bond or trust fund, you can then proceed to obtain your unified carriers registration. As a freight broker, you will need to pay a fee of $76, but for motor carriers, the amount to be said will be determined by the size of the fleet they have. A yearly registration and renewal of the fee is required by both the broker and motor carriers.

It is very easy to register for the UCR. You can register online and you can also make use of their mobile app. You can register through this link - https://www.ucr.gov/

Obtain an Insurance Coverage

The job of a freight broker is different from that of a freight forwarder. Liabilities for loss or damage during transit are usually the responsibility of the freight forwarder and rarely that of the freight broker.

But it's still best to get an insurance coverage as a broker for your protection because there are lots of risks associated with the brokerage business. You need to be fully aware of all the insurance packages for brokers, from the highest to the lowest. There are lots of insurance products out there, let take a look at some of the options out there.

General liability of property insurance – You'll need this if you want to own or lease a property.

Vicarious auto liability – This is one important insurance option for brokers in case a lawsuit is filed against you as a result of poor hiring that leads to liabilities such as the loss or damage of a cargo. This insurance option will cover a broker if he is found liable. But ensure that it can cover the size of the cargo you utilize.

Contingent cargo- it's best to have this insurance as a form of security just in case anything happens, also you don't really know the extent of the freight forwarder's policies. You are not responsible for any loss of cargo during transit, but this insurance can help fill in the gap just in case. And the basis of this insurance shouldn't be mainly legal liability.

Workers compensation – Like every other business, brokers are required by the law to have worker's compensation. Also, make sure the people you work with have workers compensation for their employees. In a case where you work with a carrier that is in a state where worker's compensation is not compulsory, they should send a written statement to you, just to exempt you from any issues with the law.

Errors and Omissions – This has nothing to do with properties or cargo loss and damage. It has to do with wrong information given by the broker unknowingly. Be sure to always check the information you give to the carrier. Because you can be charged for negligence even if it was a mistake. Basically, this insurance covers you in case something like this happens.

Make sure you get all the necessary information from a professional before purchasing any insurance. They will guide you on all the best options and decisions to make.

Chapter 6

Running of Business Operations

Every business needs some sort of management and the brokerage business is not excluded. Also, you may have lots of questions like – How much am I going to need to start this business? How do I go about it?. We are going to be helping you by answering these questions.

You will need to carefully apply wisdom when you want to start running your business. Here are a few tips that will be very helpful in running your business.

Initial Setup Expenses

This is not definite but the list we are about to provide will give you an idea of the amount of money and necessities you need as a new broker. Though your starting capital depends on a lot of factors like the location you want to use (your home or a commercial area), your desire to hire or not hire employees at the beginning and so on. Make sure your capital is sufficient to pay up your carriers and your operations for the first three months in case your shipper delays your payment.

Here is an idea of the amount you'll spend when you want to start:

- Cost of rent: $0- $1000 (you can decide to use your home hence the $0)

- Licenses/taxes: $200-$400

- Equipment:$6000-$22000

- Advertisement:$500-&1500

- Utilities: $100-$300

- Salary:$0-$5000

- Supplies: $250-$300

- Professional services:$200-$750

- Insurance: $700-$1400

Total capital you may need to have either in cash or line of credit: $5000- 250,000

You don't need to be in a hurry, you can start small and save money in the process. Getting extensive equipment or sourcing out funds to get unnecessary supplies at the beginning wouldn't help your business. Start small and grow in the process

Secure Your Initial Operation Capital

To run a freight brokerage business effectively, you will need to constantly analyze the amount you are receiving and the amount going out. The difference will let you know if you are actually gaining anything as an intermediary.

One of the things you also need to put into consideration is your ability to hold up and still pay carriers at the right time even when you haven't gotten payment from the shipper for about thirty to fifty days. For this, you can work with a factoring company to make the flow of cash steady. This will create a sustainable relationship with carriers because they are getting paid on time.

There are two different factoring options you will need to review before choosing which is best for you. They include:

Recourse Factoring – For this option, the company turns to you for reimbursement if the customer doesn't pay up. Since the company has a reduced risk, the percentage of fees is a bit low.

Non–Recourse Factoring – Here, the factoring company takes up all the responsibility concerning payment and this means the percentage fees will be really high. The higher percentage fees serve as a form of security for the factoring company.

Raising enough capital for your brokerage business.

This is usually the issue for a lot of people who aspire to start up this business. A lot of people struggle and try to do a lot yet they can't seem to get enough to start up. One of the ways to raise capital is getting investors.

Investors will always work with people who are honest, passionate and have good character. They want to see a raging desire for success. This means you can't have dishonest schemes and expect to get lasting investors.

Another way to raise capital is to get strategic partners. These partners do not just put money into the business, they also give it their all easing your stress on so many levels.

You can also consider getting a line of credit to be able to pay up carriers before you get paid by shippers.

It's advisable not to start your business with debts though, since you really don't know how fast your business will grow and your ability to generate profit within a period of time. So as not to run down your business even before it starts, consider other options first.

Essential Equipment

Even if you can't open a physical office at the beginning of your brokerage journey, there are still some important equipment you need.

At first, you'll need to get the following:

- Computer
- Copy and fax machine
- Landline and mobile number
- Printer
- Good internet
- And some basic office supplies

Getting a freight brokering software will also help improve your work and increase your productivity. You should consider getting it. As you expand in your business, you will begin to get other equipment as the need arises, but for starters, the equipment listed above are basic and are very important.

Hiring Employees

One of the key factors that will determine the longevity of your brokerage business is the employees you hire. And it's often very dicey because this can make or mar your business. A lot of people prefer to work on their own initially because they are scared of hiring the wrong people.

This can be limiting though because to grow the business effectively you will need more helping hands. There are some things you need to put into consideration when you want to hire extra hands;

1. The first question you need to ask yourself is – why do I need to hire a staff?
Having a WHY will help you know who and what you are in search of, for example, if you need someone to help in the area of marketing. You'll need to review the years of experience and qualifications of this person and sometimes all you need to see as an employer is just the burning passion even with zero years of experience. Having this understanding will help you hire the right person and keep the person focused on the main job they were hired for. To reduce the risk of losing employees, it's best to keep their tasks within the area of their expertise as adding other tasks can tire them out.

As stated earlier, they may not be seemly qualified for the position, but all you need to look out for is their character and passion. Once these two are in place, you can always train them so they can be really good at what you hired them for even in the absence of any previous experience.

2. Be smart about your decision, it's not just about having people under you, it's about having the right people you can afford under you. For example, employing a professional as an employee when you are just starting isn't really a good idea, though this may help your business boom and ease the stress of training a newbie. So you have to consider both options, what risk are you willing to take? Just make sure whoever you choose to hire is intelligent, smart, proactive and aligns with the vision of the brokerage business. That last part is important because if they do not align with your vision, they cannot really be loyal to you and you risk losing them to competitors along with your ideas, you may also lose your customers to them.

3. Be very flexible about hiring staffs, there is no point thinking too much about it. If the workload is getting so much and you need extra hands even if you initially felt the staffs you have are

sufficient, please go ahead and hire. This will help you pay attention to more important things and reduce the fatigue of excess work.

4. Another factor to consider when hiring a staff is your pocket. Can you afford an extra staff?. Make sure you have an idea of the different fee structures available so you wouldn't lose good employees because you can't pay them. You can search for employee cost before hiring new staffs, the cost includes benefit, payroll taxes, and tools or equipment needed to carry out their tasks.

5. More costs – Bringing in more people into your office will mean you need to spend more money, not just on salaries but also on equipment(desks, tables, chairs, phones, e.t.c) and maybe more office space.

   This cost we are talking about here isn't just limited to your finances. It will also cost you your time and energy, in the sense that if you have newbies you will need to spend extra time and energy training them to match up to the level of your business strength.

Additionally in the area of your time, more employees mean you will need to spend more time monitoring their job and progress.

Lastly, once you have hired more people, you'll need to understand that you are now a leader and you'll be needing new operational strategies. It's no longer a one-man business it's now an organization with a leader, you'll need an extra dose of tolerance, patience, understanding and wisdom.

Chapter 7

Establishing Your Market Audience

Niching Down Your Target Market

To succeed in any business especially as a beginner, you will need to find a niche. One of the issues new brokers face is building a solid reputation and booming financially. One of the secrets and solutions to this is finding a particular area where you can focus on and grow in. A lot of brokers want to work with every one larger brokers are servicing, which is not bad but for starters, it's best to narrow down your options

Shippers want to work with people they can trust with the safety of their load and carriers wants to work with those who pay them in full and on time. There are some shippers often overlooked by big brokers, all you need to do is source them out and start servicing them. This is called a niche, focusing on a target audience.

Little by little, your business will start booming. The amount you make may matter for each transaction, however, consistency is what keeps the business finance solid no matter how little you make for each transaction. Niche marketing is one of the secrets of growing your business as a broker.

Benefits of Niche Marketing

1. You'll have the full knowledge of your market audience. This will help you develop strategies that will help your business grow
2. Building strategies will help you develop consistency and this will breed trust and commitment from your customers
3. Trust from your customers will help you get more referrals giving you a larger network of shippers and carriers.
4. You would not lose money marketing for a larger audience that may not listen to you. Focusing on a specific group will mean you have studied them so well, so when you advertise you know the right spot to hit to get them to patronize you.

Choosing Your Niche

Now that you know the importance of having a niche, you may be wondering how do I choose a market niche?

Some freight brokers don't have a hard time getting to know their niche, it just comes naturally, while some others are not that lucky. If you have no idea of areas you'll like to focus on, here are two methods that can help you discover your niche easily.

1. Have a session with yourself and note down your skills, interest, talents and personality type and try to see the role it can play in your brokerage business.
2. Or you can just research the different areas in the industry, then choose any area you feel you can function in and develop yourself and acquire adequate knowledge on the area and how to service it effectively.

When you focus on a niche that aligns with your passion and talents, you will give it all it takes to boom. However, getting a niche is beyond just what you like, make sure any area you choose has enough growth potential so your business can grow over time.

Niche Types For Freight Brokers

There are several freight broker niches out there. Here are some areas of niches :

1. Regional niches – This means you are focusing the majority on shippers in your city or state irrespective of the product or item they ship.
2. Area of preference – This means you focus on areas you are really passionate about. For example, if you love cars so much, you can easily access their manufacturers so they can connect you to the right people.
3. Some people choose niches based on the type of trucks. Trucks like flatbeds, tankers, dry vans and so on. You can fix your focus on one or two trucks so you can get customers easily.
4. Cargo that needs extra care, with this you'll know the type of truck to use, the best season to transport and so on.

Finding Your Shipping Customers

This is one of the difficult aspects of the brokerage business. Having a steady stream of customers is very important for the growth of your business, a lot of people start out excited but end up giving up because they only get one or two shippers in a long period of time. Imagine you've put so much money into the business and you aren't getting returns, it is very disturbing and discouraging. Like every time business, you will need some strategies to grow your stream of customers. Here are some tips that can help grow your stream of customers.

1. Focus on your niche – As we've discussed previously, you need to focus on a specific area so you can grow and develop expertise in that area. It will also help you stand out, have connections, develop an endless stream of customers. From there, you can begin to spread your wings, because you already have a solid foundation.

2. Do your research – Focusing on your niche would mean you carry out adequate research on the manufacturers and suppliers in that area. You can do this by surfing the internet especially if you are completely new to the brokerage business.

3. Get registered on freight boards – You'll easily see shippers searching for carriers on these boards. You may be required to pay for some board membership, the explanation for the payment is maybe to ensure that everyone on the board is legit. Either way, you can easily find customers on several freight boards.

4. Cold calls – A lot of freight brokers avoid this because of the fear of rejection. But this is actually

one of the ways to get customers. Before you make a call, make sure you know why you are calling and have adequate knowledge about the company you are calling. With consistency even if you keep getting "No", you will eventually get a hang of it and build your stream of customers.

5. Networking – You can't grow your business by staying indoors or in a particular place. You have to network by attentions exhibits, meeting new people. Go to broker's events or functions, they may not need you now but eventually, they may have issues with the current broker they have and may need to contact you. Always drop your contact, always introduce your business, always be open to talk to others. You never know when you will get linked up.

6. The internet – We live in a world of technology, you can't expect to grow your business by just having an offline outlet or sharing handbills. You can use the internet by taking advantage of platforms like Facebook, Instagram, Linkedin, Twitter and so on. A lot of business owners have reported that many of their sales come from online customers, so you can't overlook the

internet. You will be able to reach more people online than you would offline.

Attracting Customers – What To Do

To attract customers, you will need to be at the top of your game. A lot of brokers have all it takes to have a reputable business, but the issue is they don't know how to attract customers. To attract customers you need to know what they are looking for in freight brokers. Some things shippers are looking for include:

1. Licensing – Every shipper wants to know that their loads are secure. And even if you are legit but you don't have a license, they will find it hard to trust you. So it's best to have a license from the FMCSA.

2. Multiple modes – Operating with different mode of transports can attract customers because they will feel you have it all together. So try as much as possible to get connected with carriers with different movement operations (padded van, air, train, reefers e.t.c.)

3. Legitimate carriers – Make sure you work with the right carriers. Some carriers do not have the right papers and many customers do not want to

be associated with them, so if you want a lasting business make sure your carriers have the right papers.

4. Good filing and communication system – Some customers will require some information from you and this will expose your mode of communications with carriers and also your filing system. You can use emails and other modern methods to communicate with drivers and other people involved in transactions. Also, keep your filing system organized, it will make them feel you have it all together.

5. Years of experience – This may be a bit challenging for new brokers because shippers want experienced people most times. That being said it's best not to talk about how long you've been in the business except you are asked. You can also talk about other trainings you may have done that is related to the freight broker business, if you have experienced carriers, you can chip that in too.

You can decide to work with smaller companies to build your experience, because most times these companies are willing to work with new brokers, as long as they have the right papers and the right carriers.

1. Good credit – Many customers wouldn't want to work with someone who is in debt or doesn't have good credit. They may ask questions about you around and if you are known for not paying your vendors on time, or several unpaid bills, they may not be willing to work with you. So make sure you pay bills on time.

2. Build a brand – The competition out there is rising daily, you will need something to stand out as a broker. The need for a logo cannot be over-emphasized, as it distinguishes you from others and somewhat represents what you stand for. It will make customers feel you actually know what you are doing and you have something to offer. For your logo make sure you contact professionals and communicate your need adequately, so they can create the best for you because your logo can either attract or repel your customers.

3. Join associations – There are lots of professional associations out there. Several professional associations like the Transport intermediaries

association require that you abide by some certain strict code of ethics. To customers, if you are a part of similar associations, they will feel you are serious about your business and they will love to work with you.

4. Have a website – We are in an evolving world of technology, you can't desire growth and not invest quality. You need a website to promote your business. And not just a website, but a very detailed and informative website that provides potential customers with the conviction they need to patronize you.

The end... almost!

Hey! We've made it to the final chapter of this book, and I hope you've enjoyed it so far.

If you have not done so yet, I would be incredibly thankful if you could take just a minute to leave a quick review on Amazon

Reviews are not easy to come by, and as an independent author with a little marketing budget, I rely on you, my readers, to leave a short review on Amazon.

Even if it is just a sentence or two!

So if you really enjoyed this book, please...

>> Click here to leave a brief review on Amazon.

I truly appreciate your effort to leave your review, as it truly makes a huge difference.

Chapter 8

Running Your Freight Brokerage Effectively

Handling Common Freight Brokerage Issues

It's best to know how to manage your freight brokerage effectively because it will determine how long your business will last. One of the difficult areas of this business is problem-solving. The freight brokerage business carries so much risk and problems are inevitable sometimes. In case a problem arises, you need to know how to handle such a problem without your business getting hit. Here are some common problems you will encounter and how to deal with them:

1. Sometimes carriers may be sluggish about picking up your loads. One of the ways to prevent this is to establish a relationship with them even before you need their services and also pay them on time even if you've not been paid by the shipper. Also, have a lot of carriers on your list in case a carrier does not have enough capacity to carry your load.

2. Delays – Sometimes you can't avoid this, certain factors like bad weather, technical and mechanical issues can delay a freight. All you need to do is have a good idea of time and seasons to avoid bad weather conditions and in a case where it is unavoidable, you need to constantly communicate with the customer and try as much as possible to ensure the freight gets to its destination. This will give the customers some sort of assurance and faith in you despite the delay.

3. Loss of damage of a cargo – As a freight broker, you are not responsible for any loss or damage of a cargo but it's expected that your customers will come to you. If you get complaints, contact the carrier immediately and act as the middle man between the shipper and the carrier. Making sure you do all you can in the process to resolve the issue. Ensure your carriers reads the description of every cargo especially in the area of handling to prevent damage, and they should ensure the consignee signs after receiving a cargo.

4. You can't escape one or two issues every now and then as a freight broker, but learning good

management skills will help you overcome each challenge and grow in the business.

Going Digital With Freight Broker Software

One of the ways to improve your business and remain at the top of your game is utilizing a freight broker software. Basically, this software is a management system that helps to analyze and streamline the daily operations of brokers and some other companies. Beyond being just a management system, it has features that unify the management of logistics into a single platform, at the same time keeping the company's fund safe. One of the issues freight brokers have is the large amount of data and paper works needed to keep their business organized. This can make a lot of companies look inadequate because they can't handle the information load of the different platforms they operate on.

Basically, what a freight broker software does is that it allows brokers to manage everything like shipment schedule, access inventory data, pick up appointments, viewing supply chains, viewing carrier performances, document storage and much more. This software allows you to handle everything from a remote location and even on your mobile phone.

You may be wondering how a freight broker software helps broker performance and sales.

1. It helps with better document management – There will be lots of documentation. Having a software that has a unified system will save you time, energy and effort. You wouldn't need to start visiting storage areas to search for a document.

2. Better Analytics – You can easily measure the performance of everyone involved in a transaction.

3. Automation – Automation will improve efficacy on all levels. You wouldn't need to spend time reviewing documents, or payment schemes and so much more. You can get things done in minutes.

4. Streamline payment – You wouldn't need to spend time on payment initiation, there is an integrated payment process that will automate your payment process.

Why is automation important in a freight brokerage software?

As stated above it makes the job easy for brokers, helping them maximize their time and energy. It reduces information and cost errors, it helps with full control over all transactions, improved shipment volume, it will improve your visibility as a broker, better customer care, it gives you speed, more access to accurate freight data and analysis. Overall, it gives you better organization and control. It is a really wise investment.

Conclusion

Being a freight broker is a beautiful experience. Not only do you provide job opportunities for others, most importantly, you also make other people excited. It's saddening to desire a thing and not be able to reach out for it or get it easily. The joy of having an item you have long desired at your doorstep without leaving the comfort of your home is immeasurable.

The industry is growing and you just embrace the changes that come in all areas of the sector. Ensure that you never stop learning. Take as many courses as you can. Get acquainted with the latest updates and innovations in the industry.

Finally, always ask for feedback and reviews from your client.

The information that you have absorbed from this book will take you farther and keep you at the peak of your career.

References

Casey, J. (2012, September 17). *A Brief History of the Freight Brokerage Industry*. Freight Broker Training Headquarters.

http://www.freightbrokertraininghq.com/a-brief-history-of-the-freight-brokerage-industry/

Casey, J. (2012, September 17). *A Brief History of the Freight Brokerage Industry*. Freight Broker Training Headquarters.

http://www.freightbrokertraininghq.com/a-brief-history-of-the-freight-brokerage-industry/

Casey, J. (2013, February 3). *10 Top Reasons Why You Should Become a Freight Broker Today*. Freight Broker Training Headquarters. https://www.freightbrokertraininghq.com/10-top-reasons-why-you-should-become-a-freight-broker-today/

Casey, J. (2012a, September 12). *Ultimate Guide to Being a Freight Broker - Role & Resposibilities*. Freight Broker Training Headquarters. http://www.freightbrokertraininghq.com/ultimate-guide-to-being-a-freight-broker-role-resposibilities/

Casey, J. (2013a, January 29). *Freight Broker Business Plan Template*. Freight Broker Training Headquarters. http://www.freightbrokertraininghq.com/freight-broker-business-plan-template/

ComFreight, T. (2019, May 24). *The Loading Life: How Freight Brokers Can Find Carriers Fast*. ComFreight Blog. https://blog.comfreight.com/2019/05/24/the-loading-life-how-freight-brokers-can-find-carriers-fast/

A. (2020, April 9). *Too Much Freight Broker Paperwork!* Loadpilot. https://loadpilot.com/2020/04/07/too-much-freight-broker-paperwork/

ld@dmin. (2016, December 15). *What to Consider BEFORE You Hire to Expand Your Freight Broker Business*. Logistic Dynamics, Inc. https://www.logisticdynamics.com/what-to-consider-before-you-hire-to-expand-your-freight-broker-

S. (2021, March 26). *How Freight Broker Software Increases Business Productivity*. TAI SOFTWARE. https://tai-software.com/how-freight-broker-software-increases-business-productivity/